# Chic-tionary

# Chic-tionary

The little book of fashion *faux*-cabulary

Stephanie Simons

Illustrated by Malia Carter

Skyhorse Publishing

Skyhorse Publishing books may be purchased in bulk at special discounts
for sales promotion, corporate gifts, fund-raising, or educational purposes.
Special editions can also be created to specifications. For details, contact
the Special Sales Department, Skyhorse Publishing, 307 West 36th Street,
11th Floor, New York, NY 10018 or info@skyhorsepublishing.com.

Skyhorse® and Skyhorse Publishing® are registered trademarks of
Skyhorse Publishing, Inc.®, a Delaware corporation.

Visit our website at www.skyhorsepublishing.com.

10 9 8 7 6 5 4 3 2 1

Library of Congress Cataloging-in-Publication Data is available on file.

Cover design by Malia Carter
Cover illustration by Malia Carter

Print ISBN: 978-1-62914-546-4
Ebook ISBN: 978-1-62914-902-8

Printed in China

To mom and dad, for teaching me to make up my own gibberish whenever words in the dictionary can't describe . . . and for keeping a straight face when I said I wanted to be a fashion journalist.

I love you with all of my closet (I'd say my heart, but my closet is bigger).

# A

# A

1. The cup size of the average runway model to ensure clothes hang on her body the same way they would on a wire hanger. 2. The most powerful letter in the fashion alphabet, used by *Vogue* writers to make any trend sound infinitely cooler than it really is. Example: "Pair *a* red lip and *a* smoky eye with *a* wide-leg tuxedo trouser." (Pity the fool who still uses a word like *pants* in the plural form.)

# AA

Stands for **A**laïa-holics **A**nonymous, a recovery group for celebrities who are obsessed with designer Azzedine Alaïa (a.k.a. "the king of cling") and his four-thousand-dollar bodycon dresses. AA meetings were born from the scene in *Clueless* where Cher Horowitz hesitates to comply with a robber at gun point and get down on the ground for fear it will ruin her curve-hugging Alaïa dress.

*On any given day at the Hollywood chapter of AA, you may find Alaïa devotees Mariah Carey and Kim Kardashian maintaining their lovely lady lumps with the complimentary coffee and donuts.*

## abercrumbs

Generously discounted scraps on clearance at Abercrombie & Fitch, or what's left over after all the good stuff has already been devoured by hungry teenage crowds. Abercrumbs are usually saturated in the store's pungent fragrance and available only in hard-to-pull-off colors that require a serious tan.

## abdominatrix

The *Shape* magazine cover model whose abdominal muscles make you feel completely shameful about your cart full of Frosted Flakes and Häagen-Dazs as you stand in the checkout line at the grocery store.

## abracadaver

Any hot male celebrity who—*poof!*—undergoes a significant amount of weight loss overnight in hopes of earning accolades for a movie role, channeling the same determination of women dieting for a wedding or high school reunion. The abracadaver will never seem attractive to you again, making you appreciate the joys of full cheeks and a well-placed love handle. See: *McConaughey, Matthew,* and *Bale, Christian*

## accessorcism

1. The process of taking off one piece of jewelry before you leave the house so you don't look overdone, per the sage styling wisdom of Coco Chanel. 2. What needs to happen when you feel possessed to wear every piece of jewelry you own—all at once.

*Before an important party, I look in the mirror and perform an accessorcism on myself. It's how I exorcize the mysterious entity that makes me want to decorate myself like a Christmas Tree.*

## acronymphomania

A highly contagious fashion affliction that involves the excessive use of acronyms, like *LBD* (little black dress), *LSD* (little sequin dress), *OTK* (over the knee), *OTT* (over the top), and *H2T* (head-to-toe). Editors who work at a fashion magazine for too long eventually suffer from chronic acronymphomania and refer to all their bosses, friends, and family members by their initials alone. These women are also commonly referred to as *acronymphos*. See also: *fabbrevation*

## acupcadabra

The magical way that pin-thin celebrities like Kate Hudson, Keira Knightley, and Natalie Portman never wear a bra, always rock a plunging neckline, and make the flat-chested life look amazing.

## adlerall

A soon to be FDA-approved pill that will make you a more focused, over-achieving, endlessly entertaining hostess. Named for Jonathan Adler who snagged the legendary Simon Doonan with his nesting instincts.

*The entertaining commandments:*
*Thou shalt not entertain on paper plates.*
*Thou shalt not let guests go hungry.*
*Thou shalt take Adlerall but not tell a soul.*

**adornable**

An adjective used to describe anything with the potential to look infinitely more adorable once it's adorned with the right bag, shoes, and accessories.

## adversmizing

The most illustrious form of *smizing* (a term originally coined by Tyra Banks that means smiling with your eyes) in which a celebrity is selling her perfect features on behalf of a multi-million-dollar cosmetics company.

*Charlize Theron is beyond gorgeous in the new adversmizing campaign for Dior.*

## afashionado

A fashion aficionado who knows way more about the historical intricacies of clothing and accessories than any fashion lover cares to hear. See: *Gunn, Tim*

## age-itation

A feeling of helplessness and youthlessness caused by the sudden emergence of fine lines and wrinkles seemingly overnight.

## aha moment

When you realize there's more to life than looking good, and that it's far more important to cultivate a sense of humor about these things as you age (slowly losing your vision so you can't see yourself as clearly in the mirror is just nature's protection).

## ahead-of-trend

1. The height of chicdom, sometimes resulting in ridicule. 2. A way of dress for risk-takers who enjoy wearing high stakes fashion before the native population catches on.

*Is Jane insane or just ahead-of-trend? It's honestly so hard to tell.*

**ah-choo!**

A well-timed sneeze that ever-so-subtly communicates what you really
want for your birthday.

*Ah-Choo! Ah-Choo! Ah-patent-leather-peep-toe-Jimmy-Choo!*

## aircut

A form of blow-drying that creates the illusion you got a haircut without actually sacrificing any length so you can go longer between haircuts.

## air kiss

A sophisticated type of kissing in which you pucker your lips on either side of a person's face without actually touching them. This technique allows industry people to show affection for one another, whether real or patronizing, without catching a cold, especially during flu season.

## à la model

On the model.

*Sigh. Why does everything look better à la model?*

## al desko

As in, *dining al desko* or eating at your desk by the glow of a computer screen, all slathered up with SPF to prevent premature photo-aging, as most full-time beauty editors do. See also: *dot com damage*

## a-line personality

Used to describe any designer with an easily flared, slightly tapered temper.

## alpha hydroxy male

A modern alpha man who's as aggressive about his skincare routine as he is in the boardroom.

## altar ego

The phenomenon in which a bride looks completely different than her usual self—for better or worse—at the altar on her wedding day.

## amateur night

Christmas Eve, when the inexperienced, uninitiated shoppers of the world are out in full effect, slowing down the mall regulars and hogging their designated parking spaces.

## amaze-za-za-zing

1. The highest possible compliment, used to describe how a woman looks when amazing isn't enough. 2. A hybrid of the words *amazing* and *zsa-zsa-zsu*, originally coined by Carrie Bradshaw to describe love at first sight.

## ambien alert

The equivalent of an Amber Alert: an office-wide emergency response system that's used to notify *Vogue* coworkers when an unpaid intern goes missing (e.g., is taking a nap in the accessories closet) due to improper use of self-prescribed insomnia meds.

*Okay, it's 8:35 a.m. and we can't start the meeting without our champion coffee-maker. Sound the Ambien Alert!*

## angel hair straps

Slightly more delicate than spaghetti straps and guaranteed to break if you raise the roof on the dance floor.

## angling

Fishing for your best angle in photos, especially selfies.

## anistone

The most luminous shade of golden-blond that's neither too brassy nor too ashy, named for Jennifer Aniston's sun-kissed locks.

## annedroid

Any starlet so awkwardly geeky or over-rehearsed she seems alien on the red carpet, named for Anne Hathaway.

## apocalypstick

The new lipstick you don't need but buy anyway to make yourself feel better under severe end-of-the-world-ish stress.

## après-sex hair

A coveted hairstyle that aims to achieve a just-rolled-out-of-bed-with-Liam-Hemsworth look.

## armenian tuxedo

Kind of like a Canadian tuxedo, but instead of head-to-toe denim, head-to-toe body hair. Kim Kardashian is said to have had her Armenian tuxedo permanently removed with lasers.

## arm party

The official term for stacking a bunch of different bracelets on the same arm in all manner of materials, metals, and colors as though you got dressed while drunk. The more bracelets the merrier; hence the popularity of the *raging double-fisted arm party* in which both arms are accessorized from wrist to elbow. This term was originally coined by *Man Repeller,* a blog devoted to the art of dressing for no one but yourself, even if it means baffling the entire male species.

**arm party crasher**

The name for any clueless person who kills your style buzz by asking things like, "Why are you wearing so many bracelets on one arm at one time?" and "What on Earth are you wearing?"

*I want to wear my new Miss Cleo–inspired turban to my parent's dinner, but my brother's such an arm party crasher, I think I'll save it for another occasion.*

## arse whisperer

A celebrity trainer who tames a big, wild booty though a series of exercises and gentle encouragement. See: *Peterson, Gunnar*

## artificial inseamination

The process of taking an ill-fitting garment to a seamstress to turn it into something nobody else on the planet will ever own.

*This was a blazer before the artificial inseamination. Now I'm the proud parent of a one-of-a-kind vest.*

## asspiration

A divine booty influence whose picture may or may not be taped on the front of your refrigerator to get you to the gym. See: *Biel, Jessica*

## ATM

A multi-billion-dollar husband who insists on having a joint shopping account and letting his Dior-digging wife go on the kind of buying sprees that could single-handedly turn around a recession.

## ATM withdrawls

What the aforementioned Dior Digger experiences after being divorced by said ATM.

## atomic blond

A shade of platinum so unnatural and so nuclear it should only be administered by an official wearing a hazmat suit in a national security laboratory in Livermore, California.

## attachment disorder

A condition that involves leaving the tags on clothes for immediate return to the store after wearing them. Be forewarned: karma will always get you in the form of a giant salsa stain.

## avant-garde-ning

The process of snipping and waxing your nether topiary into the shape of a designer monogram, a naughty little trend inspired by Tom Ford's banned Gucci ads.

## awards ward

A special unit of the insane asylum where celebrities like Björk are admitted after wearing a red carpet ensemble that screams "I've gone freaking nuts!" to the world. Here they also receive intensive treatment for any damage to their ego that may have been caused by Joan Rivers's jokes on *Fashion Police*.

B

## bad hair year

Exponentially worse than a bad hair day, a bad hair year occurs after a botched cut and entails 365 days of buns, barrettes, hats, headbands, and hairpieces. It is, however, far less unfortunate than a bad hair lifetime, which is totally genetic.

## bad nair day

What transpires when you depilate yourself and miss some pretty important spots. See also: *fuzzkill*

## bagism

A form of discrimination directed at someone with a "lesser" purse.

## bag-gressive

A term used to describe a woman who carries an enormous purse in anticipation of needing to push her way through a large crowd.

## bag hag

Someone who only wears hideously expensive bags and believes she's a better person for it. See also: *sackreligious*

## baguetto (pronounced "bag ghetto")

A sketchy neighborhood where you can buy a knock-off Fendi baguette out of the trunk of a Cadillac.

## bakeover

*Vive la différence* a bottle of self-tanning lotion can make overnight.

## bananas

Might mean crazy-bad or crazy-good, depending. Rachel Zoe uses this term in every interview she's ever given.

## banano-second

The time elapsed between the moment you buy a cashmere cardi for full price at Banana Republic and the moment it goes on sale when you walk out the door.

## bandage dress

Like full-body Spanx for all the world to see. See: *Léger, Hervé*

## banglish

Special sign language using the thumb and forefinger to accurately communicate how many millimeters you'd like trimmed from your bangs, since most hairstylists don't own a metric ruler and somehow have their own perceptions of what constitutes an inch, depending on their mood.

## bangover

The morning-after remorse that occurs after getting bangs that are too short and don't behave.

## bangry

An emotion that can drive you to cut your own bangs in an impulsive fit of rage as a cry for help. See also: *Lorena Bobbitry*

*I was so bangry last night I almost did something regrettable!*

## bathroom stalling

Escaping to the ladies room to powder your nose, clip your cuticles, put on a Crest Whitestrip, or engage in any other beauty regimen that kills time to avoid an awkward situation.

## bathtermath

Massive prunage of fingers and toes that results from catching up on your favorite fashion magazine while soaking in the tub.

## bauble head

The fashion equivalent of an air head: a person who's easily distracted by your pretty, shiny baubles, often interrupting you mid-sentence during important conversations just to compliment your *"oooooh pretty!"* jewelry.

## BBTS

**B**ored **b**y **t**hose **s**hoes, because nothing ruins a strong look faster than a pair of basic black pumps.

## BC

**B**efore **C**arrie (on *Sex and the City*).

*Women in New York were wearing Manolos ten thousand years BC.*

## BDD

**B**udget **d**eficit **d**isorder, or the inability to focus and stay within your monetary means while shopping.

## beach-slap

An extreme form of sunburn that will prevent you from wearing anything tweed for a very long time.

## beachy hair

Undulating waves that appear as if your hair was enviably knotted by a violent ocean breeze when really you tortured it yourself in the bathroom.

## beau-hemian

1. A boyfriend who dresses boho to the point of looking homeless, which instantly makes you appear cooler by association. 2. The preferred significant other for fashionistas like Kate Moss.

## bebe pellets

Annoying little beads, sequins, and pailettes that always seem to pop off Bebe's provocatively slinky sequin dresses every time you try to squeeze into them.

## bedroom eyes

Commonly known as smoky eyes, and achieved with copious amounts of black eyeshadow to create the appearance of sockets so sultry.

### beiberhood

Another name for Robertson Boulevard in Los Angeles, a neighborhood
with so much celebrity spotting going on you choose to shop there over
Melrose (which is so much more eclectic), just for the star thrills. Because,
let's face it, it's kind of pathetic to return from a SoCal vacation without
seeing Justin Beiber or Selena Gomez in the flesh.

## bells yeah!

A celebratory phrase marking the triumphant return of
Florence Henderson–inspired high-waisted flares every few years.

## bergdork

The sales girl at Bergdorf Goodman who knows far less about the skincare
product she's selling than you do.

*When dealing with a Bergdork, it's best to ask for a supervisor.*

## beyond

Something so infinitely awesome it's hard to find words to describe it.

## bible

1. *Vogue* magazine, the holiest of scriptures decreeing the tenants for
proper dress. 2. A phrase meaning "swear to God," as uttered every fifteen
seconds by the Kardashian sisterhood and Kris Jenner.

## bilbro baggins

A vertically challenged bro who you decide to date until you realize how
much you miss wearing high heels. Named for Bilbo Baggins, a hobbit
from the Shire in *The Lord of the Rings*.

## bill blassphemy

Lack of reverence for Bill Blass, the original American fashion designer
who defined relaxed, pared-down elegance long before Michael Kors.

## birking

To wear Birkenstocks (at your own risk).

### birkin stalking

Going to scary, stalker-ish extremes (such as lying, like Samantha Jones on *Sex and the City*) with the intent to score a coveted four-figure Hermès Birkin bag.

## birth control-top panty hose

Another term for control-top panty hose, which moonlights as a lower body prophylactic since it's certain to kill the mood if discovered by a man's wandering hands. See also: *drabotage*

*Remind me to refill my birth control-top panty hose to keep my date at a reasonable distance.*

## birthright

That particular right every woman is bestowed at birth, which includes but is not limited to clear skin and shiny hair if you take proper care.

## bitch face

Also affectionately known as chronic resting bitch face, bitch face makes you seem unfriendly even though you feel like a ray of sunshine on the inside, which is imperative for working in fashion and being taken seriously. You'll know if you have it, because you'll find yourself constantly reassuring people you're not mad at them or hearing they thought you were a total bitch when they first met you even though you're an angel. Models with bitch face are obviously much easier to hate; some spend their whole lives trying to perfect the look. Paired with the right pantsuit and heels, bitch face can be fiercely fabulous and will help you keep away the wrong kind of men on the subway. See also: *terminal chillness*

## bi-textural

How to describe hair that's unsure it wants to be straight and occasionally swings kinky.

## black

1. A sartorial safety net. Wear it when you feel fat, depressed, or lacking imagination. 2. Fashion's strangest analogy, as in "[blank] is the new black" or stranger yet, "black is the new black." (Yes, this was once written in a fashion mag that will remain anonymous.)

## blahnik fatigue syndrome

A condition caused by standing in ill-fitting Manolo Blahnik heels all day. So worth it.

## blemishphere

Another term for the T-zone (a facial hemisphere that encompasses the forehead, nose, and chin), which is prone to excess oil production and eruptions rivaling Mauna Loa when you're under stress.

## blondsequences

The laundry list of consequences that only a skilled colorist will warn you about when you impulsively decide you want to go blond. A trusted professional will always tell you that your hair will probably never be the exact shade you want, that you must be prepared to deep condition every two hours, and that you will inevitably spend your rent money on root upkeep.

## blondstipation

The uncomfortable "stuck" feeling that brunettes with golden undertones experience after spending a lot of money to go blond and leaving the salon looking red-orange or only halfway there.

## blondtroversy

The social panic that occurs when a long time brunette (think Kate Beckinsale) or redhead (Laura Prepon) goes blond.

## blowbotomy

When you emerge from the blow-dry bar feeling like a new, improved person.

## blowcasion

Any special occasion, such as a date with George Clooney, that justifies spending fifty dollars on a professional blow-dry.

## blowcation

A much-needed vacation from your hair-dryer and other heated styling tools. See also: *spare the hair day*

## BNB

Stands for **b**angs **n**ot **b**otox, a cruelty-free anti-aging mantra that encourages women to forgo Botox for more creative hairstyling options to hide the frown lines between their eyes.

## bobligation

The imaginary "obligation" to society that causes some women to cut their hair into a bob once they turn a certain age.

## BOJO

Stands for **b**emoan **o**ne **j**ob, get **o**ne free, based on the shopping concept of BOGO or "buy one get one free." It means doing the jobs of at least two people at one time, best understood by anyone who's ever worked in retail marketing and now has a nervous twitch in one eye.

*I was duped! I should have known this was a BOJO operation by the way the hiring manager responded to my emails at 1 a.m.*

## boobiesitter

An appointed guardian who looks after one or more of your boobs when you're inebriated or otherwise unable to tell whether they're spilling out of your tube top. See also: *titastrophe*

## boobonic plague

An epidemic native to Los Angeles, Dallas, and Miami wherein a majority of the population are bitten by a bug that causes them to purchase silicone amenities that are way too big for their bodies and spaced way too far apart.

## boomerang ring

A promise, engagement, or wedding ring you receive after it's already been gifted to someone else (also spelled *g-r-o-s-s*).

## booty-tooching

The act of sticking out your tush to eliminate stomach pooch and look more alluring in photos, as coined by Tyra Banks.

## born-again fashionista

1. What you become the day you wake up and realize life's too short to wear boring clothes. 2. A person with a renewed faith in fashion or sudden devotion to looking put-together, usually brought on by a new job or weekend makeover movie.

**bottega vendetta**

Sweet revenge achieved by dressing well, the cherry on top being an expensive bag by Bottega Veneta.

**boyfriend cleanse**

Detoxing your wardrobe of boyfriend trends that don't do your figure any favors, like oversized jeans and Mr. Rogers–style cardigans.

**bracelets on**

A phrase meaning "I'm dressed to kill and ready to roll, with every last ring and accessory in perfect place."

**bra dysmorphic syndrome**

A condition caused by the wrong bra, which distorts your clothing in a way that makes your body appear to have back fat or uniboob.

**brathel**

A place that sells skanky undergarments.

**brastitute**

A person who shops at said brathel and is unafraid to let her leopard-and rhinestone-studded bra straps become the focal point of her outfit.

## bratrayal

When your brassiere straps uncomfortably dig into your shoulders, or worse, totally stab you in the back.

## brazilianaire

A female who wins the genetic lottery at birth and spends the rest of her life making millions of dollars modeling after being discovered on a beach in her native Brazil (without makeup). See: *Bündchen, Gisele*

## breakover

A makeover fueled by an ugly breakup.

## breastcapade

A night on the town with a group of single girlfriends who show a lot of cleavage to attract the opposite sex. See also: *vajaycay*

## brokeback acne

A form of back acne caused by incessant, sweaty spooning with a man who just can't quit you.

## browhab

A break from tweezing to grow out self-inflicted mistakes.

*I'm in browhab right now; you can't expect me to look in a magnifying mirror. That's like putting a beer in front of an alcoholic.*

## brunetiquette

The etiquette of letting blondes believe they have more fun when that's simply not true.

## BS

Stands for **b**ikini **s**eason.

*I can't eat donut holes again until September. This is BS!*

**bugly**

Used to describe windshield-sized sunglasses that make you resemble a
large insect that needs to be swatted.

## bullchic

Linguistic fashion fluffery with no real meaning, as mastered by American fashion writers who use the word *chic* with reckless abandon, often pairing it with ambiguous adjectives and nouns to create all kinds of winning combinations (*profoundly chic, achingly chic, impossibly chic, devastatingly chic, geek-chic, yeti-chic, prison-chic).*

## bumpsuit

A maternity jumpsuit.

## bunundrum

To top knot or not to top knot? That is the question when you haven't washed your hair in three days.

## burberry jam

A mad dash to the Burberry store when you get off work, hopefully before it closes.

## butt glue

A form of adhesive that pageant contestants use to keep their bikini bottoms from wandering; not to be confused with butt paste, which is for babies with diaper rash.

## butter butt

The opposite of *butter face:* a person who's really attractive except for a very questionable-looking rear end, a product of wearing saggy sweatpants or booty-flattening jeans.

## burbie doll

Another term for a suburban Barbie. A look that's popular among real plastic housewives who live in Orange County.

## bustache

The stray hairs that sometimes grow around a woman's nipples that nobody wants to talk about. Moving on . . .

## buy accident

When you buy something you weren't looking for just because your wallet happens to be open and you're awake.

*Girl 1: Cute shoes!*
*Girl 2: Thanks, I got them buy accident!*

## buyagra

A soon to be FDA-approved pill you can pop to increase your shopping stamina.

## buy-arreah

Uncontrollably buying things without regard for your budget.

## buy caramba!

An exclamation used to denote frustration when you can't figure out which fall essential is more essential.

*The chunky knit cardi or the knee-high boots? Buy caramba!*

## buy-curious

"Just browsing, thanks."

## buygraine

A throbbing salesperson-induced headache.

## buyjacking

The process of interfering with another woman's purchase by snapping it up first.

## buy-polar disorder

The impulse to purchase things—glorious things!—followed by an immediate desire to return them once you get them home. See also: *returning spree*

*I'm being more careful about what I purchase now that I know I'm buy-polar.*

## buysexual

Someone for whom the love of shopping is downright fetishist.

## BUI

1. **B**uying **u**nder the **i**nfluence of alcohol. 2. Buying under the influence of a friend who says everything looks great on you.

**buyceps**

Muscles developed from carrying heavy shopping bags.

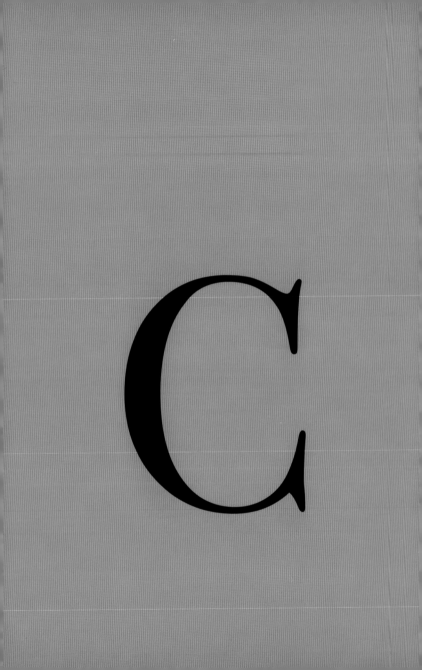

## cakeup

Thick foundation resembling marzipan frosting, possibly applied with a
pastry knife. See also: *VFL (visible foundation line)*

## cabbing it

The only way to travel more than fifty yards in your Louboutins.

## canyon cleav

Cleavage that has an echo because its depths rival the Grand Canyon.

## carb footprint

The unfortunate aftereffects of eating too many carbs in one sitting, including the repercussions they have on your waistline.

## carpe denim

A phrase meaning "seize the *day-um!* girl" in those skin-tight jeans.

*Girl 1: I've got a date tonight.*
*What should I wear?*
*Girl 2: Carpe denim!*

## cashmerde

Sh*tty, inexpensive cashmere, derived from the French word *merde*.

## cashtastrophe

What happens when a store is cash only, rendering your checkbook and credit cards useless and sending you on the prowl for the nearest automated teller machine.

## cashventurous

A person who buys things she can't afford just to get an adrenaline rush at the register.

## casualty friday

The one day a week that gives you a fleeting, and totally uncomfortable, glimpse of what your coworkers really dress like outside of the office.

## celebeauty

An unattainable standard of beauty set by celebrities who deny they've had any work done and make you feel haggard by comparison. See also: *skinspiracy*

## celebutaunt

Criticism of a star's outfit.

## cell esteem

A sudden boost of confidence bestowed by pretending to be on an important call with Karl or Oscar while walking into a fashion party alone.

## cellufright

The fear of cellulite and the harsh fitting room lighting that intensifies it. See also: *lipochondria*

*I don't know what it is about the lighting in Nordstrom fitting rooms, but it totally exacerbates my cellufright. I prefer to try on swimsuits in the dark, thank you very much.*

## chanel-retentive

A term used to describe snooty salespeople who obviously never saw *Pretty Woman* and unfavorably look you up and down like a dirty street pigeon because they think you can't afford whatever they're selling.

## chairity

The selfless act of giving up a front-row seat at a show to a deserving intern.

*Chairity is a very noble act, but we've yet to see it happen at Fashion Week.*

## champers

Champagne.

## chic

1.) The most unimaginative, overused word in fashion. 2.) A highly subjective word that means "stylish."

## chiccups

Involuntary spasms in the diaphragm caused by tourniquet-tight, hourglass-enforcing undergarments.

## chic disturber

Someone in your life who continually raises the bar with her choice of wardrobe and has a subtle way of making you feel just-rolled-out-of-bed by comparison.

## chic ethic

1. Like work ethic, but pertaining to personal style. 2. The principle that one should uphold a certain wardrobe standard and stick to it at all times, even when no one's looking.

*Jane got hired because of her chic ethic. Her style never takes a sick day.*

## chic for brains

Someone who knows everything about fashion but nothing about news headlines in the real world.

## chiffontourage

A gaggle of bridesmaids wearing the same chiffon dress, also known as *taffeta mafia*.

## citizens of humanity arrest

1. A form of arrest that empowers ordinary everyday citizens to stop perpetrators from committing very serious denim crimes, like camel toe. 2. An important part of fashion law enforcement.

## chooicide

Killing your feet, and likely your chances for a second date, by wearing inappropriately tall Choos you can't actually walk in, thus preventing you from being any fun all night.

## CIB

Stands for **c**rying **i**n the **b**athroom, the fashion office equivalent of MIA (or "missing in action").

## clackers

Coworkers whose stiletto heels make a clacking sound in the hallway at the office. (The good news is they can never sneak up on you while you're shopping at your computer.) Originally coined by *The Devil Wears Prada.* See related: *stilecho*

## classic

What something becomes if it hangs around long enough.

## cleaver fever

A Hollywood phenomenon that involves undergoing the knife to look younger than you did fifteen years ago *à la* Benjamin Button.

## click-clique

A group of best-dressed socialites named for the sound the cameras make when they're photographed together at all the hottest parties.

## cliptomania

An obsession that involves snipping your hair a little each day to prevent it from growing out.

*Every day in art class, twelve-year-old Cate would take craft scissors to her bangs, an early sign of cliptomania.*

## closet envy

In Freudian psychoanalysis, this refers to the theorized reaction of a girl who suddenly realizes she is not the best-dressed woman in the room.

## closet rich

Wealth measured by the clothes hanging in your closet.

*It's perfectly possible to be closet rich, even if you're cash poor.*

## closing voice

The sudden change of pitch or tone in a sales person's voice when 1.) they think they are about to close a sale or 2.) the store is closing and they want you to leave so they can go home.

## clothestrophobia

Fear of not having enough closet space, also known as *shelf-consciousness.*

## clutter bug

1. The opposite of a litter bug. 2. Used to describe a woman who treats her purse like a trash receptacle to stash gum wrappers, receipts, and other junk she was kind enough not to litter on the side of the road.

### coachella de vil

The evil, wealthy antagonist who brags on Facebook and Twitter about all of the Coachella adventures you missed out on this year. Move over, Cruella de Vil.

### coif medicine

The prescription for misbehaving hair: frizz serum.

### comatoes

Lower body numbness caused by wearing open toe shoes in the dead of winter.

### cord ordinance

Town-issued legislation that prevents your neighbors from disrupting your peace, e.g., when you look out your window and see them gardening in worn-in cords that are mud splattered and droopy in the rear.

### CPH

Kind of like the Cost Per Wear (CPW) equation, but used to measure Compliments Per Hour. Just another mathematical means of justifying scandalously expensive purchases.

### conniption fitting

A fitting room meltdown caused by a succession of less-than-perfect wedding dresses, swimsuits, or other garments of dire importance.

## cop a frill

To take the liberty of groping gorgeous items on display.

*I know I'm on a budget, just let me pop in Kate Spade for a second to cop a frill.*

## copycattiness

The filthiest form of spite wherein another woman copies your look after making fun of it.

## cosmo-sis

A phenomenon that causes women working at *Cosmo* magazine to all begin to look and sound alike and actually *become* the magazine by process of osmosis.

## cougar toe

A direct descendant of camel toe, most commonly spotted on cougars in the wild wearing skin-tight leather jumpsuits.

## coutourture

Extreme punishment inflicted by high-end clothing you're afraid to eat, drink, or sit down in.

## crave cave

Your closet.

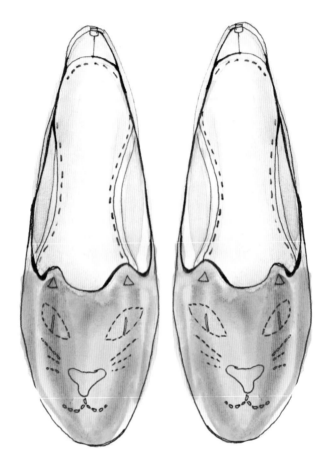

**crazy catwalk lady**

A derogatory term for an aging spinster supermodel who trades in her
rock star husband for many cats, replaces her red carpet wardrobe with
pajamas and slippers, and now subsists happily in front of the tv watching
reruns of *America's Next Top Model.*

# C·R·E·A·M

# CASHMERE RULES EVERYTHING AROUND ME.

### CREAM

Acronym for **c**ashmere **r**ules **e**verything **a**round **m**e, based on the
Wu Tang Clan song "Cash Rules Everything Around Me."
Dolla dolla bill, yo.

## credit cardiac arrest

A condition caused by excessive card activity and best treated by a credit cardiologist.

## credit conscience

The little voice that tells you to step away from something you don't really need while shopping.

## cringe and purge

1. A super-intensive form of closet cleaning that causes a person to cringe and/or cry. 2. What happens on *What Not to Wear* as Clinton Kelly and Stacy London expunge everything hideous from people's wardrobes. See also: *purge-gatory*

## cringey

A slightly lesser offense than creepy.

*Liz's red pleather pants are so cringey. Does she know we can see what she had for dinner?*

## cropaganda

Any photo cropped with the intention of misleading the general public (this includes, but is not limited to, cropping off your legs because they didn't look tan enough, cropping off your arms because they look fat, or cropping off the top of a bad hair day).

## crowbar

A must for getting into those super tight skinny jeans.

## cryliner

Mega-waterproof eyeliner that's meant to be worn when you predict a PMS-induced skirmish with your boyfriend/mother/random stranger coming on.

## curlfriends

A group of gal pals on the same follicular wave length and forever bonded by their flat irons.

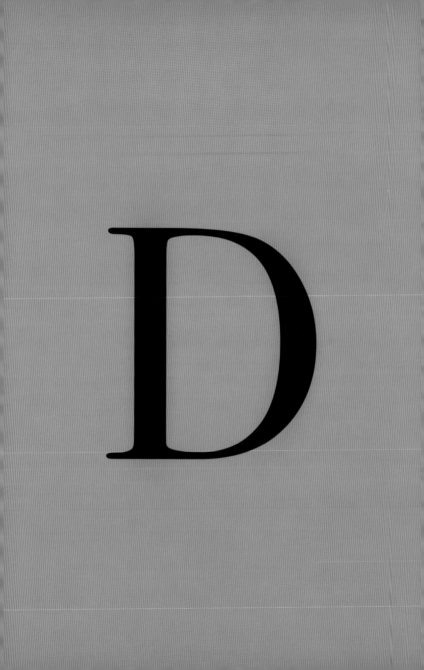

**dearly departed soles**

Shoes given away on consignment that you miss on occasion.

**debt lag**

A temporary disruption of bodily rhythms caused by spending more than you meant to on vacation.

**the debt set**

A group of people whose jet-set lifestyle has made them broke.

**de la rental**

A fashionable way of saying your designer bag is borrowed.

*Don't spill your cocktail on my de la Rental.*

**déjà mumu**

What's happening when a tent-like floral dress suddenly reminds you of your grandmother's sofa.

**dental illness**

As suffered by 1 in 3 pageant contestants who don't believe their teeth are white enough.

**department score**

A reasonably priced find that's even cheaper than you expected at the register and further reduced when you use your Macy's card.

*Hattie: Love your purse!*
*Maddie: Thanks, total department score.*

**dermaggedon**

The panic that ensues when your dermatologist tells you to just leave it alone and it will go away by itself in six to twelve weeks.

**dermatalogical clock**

What's silently ticking away beneath your skin's surface, until one day you turn a certain age and all the sun damage starts to surface.

**destresscapade**

A well-deserved day of pampering at the spa.

**detoxicated**

The feeling of becoming too quickly intoxicated after just one drink following a detox, diet, or cleanse.

## diorganization

The process of alphabetizing your closet by labels to keep it from feeling like one big designer compost pile.

## diorgasm

What happens while shopping when you encounter something Dior that lights up all the pleasure centers of your brain and makes you breathe heavily like a scene out of *9½ Weeks*.

## diva-vorce

The legal dissolution of binding contracts between a Hollywood diva and her manager.

## DIY-UI

**D**oing **i**t **y**ourself or attempting to operate sewing machinery **u**nder the **i**nfluence. See also: *sewbriety test*

## donor eyebrows

Temporary brows, created with a pencil, that will help you buy time until your real ones grow back.

## donatellavision

Kind of like tunnel vision, except it's when a guy only has eyes for the woman in the room with the blondest hair, tannest skin, most pronounced cheek bones and biggest lips/boobs. So named for the extremely unnatural look Donatella Versace has made famous.

*Ever since I broke up with my ex, it's like he has Donatellavision and only dates the most ridiculous-looking women on the planet.*

### dopplebanger

Someone who resembles someone else, but only because of her hairstyle, especially if bangs are involved.

*Julie frequently gets mistaken for Zooey Deschanel, but upon closer inspection, she's really just her dopplebanger.*

## dot com damage

The new sun damage, caused by hours logged in front of a computer screen.

## drabotage

Making yourself completely drab beneath your clothes (i.e., wearing ratty old underwear) to avoid emotional complications and minimize your chances of hooking up with a guy.

*Suze totally drabotaged herself and it backfired when she drank too much on her date with Rob and let him grope her anyway.*

## dreckitude

A hybrid of the words *wreck, dreck,* and *attitude,* used to describe something dreadful or over-hyped, particularly as it pertains to the art of modeling. See also: *shrekitude*

## dressaster

When your favorite frock becomes stained or unhitched at the straps during an important event.

## dressed to spill

A phrase meaning "wearing old clothes," mostly used by mothers in the presence of babies who might spill, poop, or spit up at any given time.

## dresslexia

A condition that involves leaving the house with your clothes on backwards for any number of reasons including power failure or sheer carelessness.

### dresspassing

When another woman invades your territory by showing up in the same dress as you.

### dresspionage

What's going on when "a friend" calls to ask what you're wearing tonight: she wants to one-up you.

### dressercize

The accidental workout you get from any frock requiring you to constantly suck in your stomach, squeeze your buns, or lug around twenty pounds of beading all night long.

### dresstiny

Wearing the right thing at the right time and getting photographed in it for all of society to see.

### drinking and drying

The impossible process of painting your own nails while wine drunk and resisting the urge to flail your arms, open a box of cookies, or touch anything within reach while you wait for them to dry.

### drive-by shoe-ing

When a stranger yells out that she loves your shoes as she whisks by you on the street without stopping to ask where you got them.

### drop a rib

To lose five pounds, preferably overnight, as suggested by modeling agents to healthy-looking women who dream of becoming cover girls.

*"If you drop a rib, wear less eye makeup, learn how to slouch, and cut off your long hair, we might think about signing you," said the model scout.*

### dry clean only

Total pain in the ass.

### drugstore cartel

Any drug store, such as a CVS or Walgreens, that promotes your addiction to reasonably priced makeup and skincare. See also: *makeuppers*

### duran duran-druff

A form of dandruff that's caused by flaky hair product (named for the '80s hair band Duran Duran).

**dye-arrhea**

The process of dying your hair to Rainbow Bright extremes to keep up with Katy Perry.

**eclipstick**

A screaming shade of lipstick so bold it diverts attention from bad hair
days, breakouts, and boring conversation.

**ediphile**

A person with a subscription to every major fashion magazine.

*If only most dentists and gynecologists were ediphiles, waiting around in their lobbies for hours would be a lot more enjoyable.*

**e!piphany**

The revelation that life's too short to stay home watching *Keeping Up with the Kardashian* reruns on the E! Network.

**era-sistible**

How to describe something that will forever be in style, no matter what decade. See also: *regret me nots*

**ESL**

**E**berjay as **s**econd **l**anguage.

**ex-boyfriend jeans**

A term of endearment for boyfriend jeans that are *so over.*

**exchangel**

The heaven-sent store manager who allows you to make an exchange even though it's a few days past a store's thirty-day return policy.

**eew!**

A little shriek of horror meant to convey playful hatred.

*"Eew! She got the newest Prada bag before me!"*

### eyebrow truth

A universal truth that all females hold to be self-evident: that you can tell a lot about another woman's mental state by her eyebrows.

*According to the eyebrow truth, my ex's new girlfriend is wacko. I give them six months, tops.*

## fabbreviation

The process of amputating a word beyond any immediate recognition to make it sound more fabulous (e.g., present becomes *prezzie*, gorgeous becomes *gorge*). Fabbreviation saves time talking, so you can spend more time being in more important places with celebs like SJP, ScarJo, J-Law, and LiLo. Totes brill, no?

## fabrication

A pretentious way of saying fabric, typically used to describe menswear and bamboozle you into buying the generic and overpriced.

## fabstinence

The conscious decision to refrain from being fabulous to uncomplicate your love life.

## fabstract

How to describe any trend that's dubiously fabulous or so foreign to men it needs an interpreter (like wedge sneakers: you're not sure if you love them or hate them, but have to have them anyway).

## fabsolute

The end-all-be-all of without-a-doubt, beyond-a-cure fabulosity.
See also: *is everything*

## fatchel

A satchel in desperate need of a diet because it weighs ninety pounds due to being stuffed with everything you own. See also: *hunchback*

## fauxbesity

1. When a pair of jeans makes you look fatter than you really are.
2. The reason why perfectly sane women ask, "Does this make my butt look big?"

*Approximately 1 in 5 Americans are fauxbese.*

## fauxtesque

Something so obviously fake its grotesque.

## fauxtographer

A creep who pretends to be a photographer for the sake of picking up models.

## fashion fauxcabulary

1. A super-exclusive language understood only by the truly stylish.
2. A collection of perfect little words you can rely on when real ones just won't do. 3. What comprises this entire book.

### fashion no show

Made completely obvious by the empty chair in the front row.

### fashion weep

What immediately follows Fashion Week when the tents come down and the eerie quietude sets in all over New York.

### fashist regime

A form of editorial dictatorship where there's no room for anyone else's opinion because one editrix overrules all and uses her power as an instrument of oppression. See: *Priestly, Miranda*

### fendi bender

Another term for going hog wild at a Fendi boutique.

### fête-abolism

The phenomenon in which calories consumed while standing and making small talk at a *fête* (the French word for party) do not count.

### fifty shades of cray

Used to describe any person (usually a rockstar) who has a wardrobe of ridiculously obnoxious sunglasses.

### fingertipsy

A state of intoxication caused by inhaling nail polish fumes and reading tabloid mags in a poorly ventilated salon.

### fit it then quit it

To try something on and not bother hanging it up when you're done, also known as *fit and run.*

### fitting room rage

The use of expletives and finger gestures caused by a mile-long traffic jam of other shoppers also waiting to try on clothes at H&M on a Saturday afternoon.

### fiscally enraged

An emotion commonly associated with tax season if you stop to think about how many shoes you could have purchased with the money you owe the IRS.

### flaccid reflux

The process of regurgitating last night's dinner upon seeing a man in a Speedo emerging from cold water.

### flammable

1. Easily set on fire. 2. How an otherwise fresh-faced woman looks after applying an entire can of liquid paint to her skin.

### flannel surfer

1. What one becomes when one is depressed, possibly after comparing one's self to too many glossy fashion magazines. 2. Another name for a couch potato who lives in her flannel pajamas and only gets up to refill the Doritos or answer the door for the guy delivering her online shoppings.

## flats-ulence

The squeaky sound new, rubber-soled ballet flats make on a linoleum floor, causing you much embarrassment.

*Calm down, people, that wasn't me. Just some flatsulence. You can stop holding your breath.*

## floral fixation

A condition in which a person is obsessed with floral prints and wears them all the time. (Unfortunately, the mere sight of this person may aggravate your allergies.)

## flubberghasted

Astonishment beyond all belief that you can no longer fit into certain jeans. Blame it on the dryer.

## fly-buy

A purchase made at top speed, usually on a lunch hour or between conference calls.

## flying squirrel wings

1. Another term for bingo wings. 2. A pendulous spread of flabby upper armskin that could help you fly from treetop to treetop if only you were a small woodland creature. 3. The inspiration for batwing sleeves.

## FOBO

**F**ear **of b**reaking **o**ut, usually experienced in the days leading up to a very important event.

## FOMO

**F**ear **of m**axing **o**ut (your credit card).

*Remind me never to go to another Half Yearly Sale again. The FOMO is too much to bear.*

## frame whore

A term used to describe the girl at work whose desk is directly across from yours and adorned with a picture of her boyfriend, which would be fine if it didn't change every week. *Frame whores* are most commonly found working at fashion and beauty brands where a high ratio of employees are female, causing them to seek out testosterone in high doses.

## freakum dress

The hot little number you reach for when you want to turn heads or are expecting an evening of *dancefloornication*, as rhapsodized by Beyoncé.

## frêt-à-porter

The fear of wearing brand new clothes, especially anything that's dry-clean only.

## frequent buyer miles

Rewards accumulated through the use of a credit card.

## frillbilly

A backwoods babe who churns her own Shea butter, totes a 'coon skin clutch, and can make a gown out of a gunnysack. See also: *Miss Arkansas USA*

### frillosopher

Any person who believes 'tis better to be overdressed.

*Oscar Wilde is one of the greatest frillosophers of our time.*

### frock bottom

A new low achieved when someone shows up in an unthinkable dress.

### frocket

An amazing dress (think Elizabeth Hurley's safety pin frock) with the power to catapult a semi-famous starlet's career into the stratosphere in the snap of a camera flash.

### frock o'clock

The hour at which evening attire becomes appropriate.

*Hell yes I'm wearing sequins in the daytime; it's frock o'clock somewhere.*

### f\*\*ck me pumps

Shoes that do all the slutting for you.

### fug-o-war

A friendly game of self-deprecation between women that turns into a full-fledged battle over who looks the worst.

*Karen Smith: God. My hips are huge!*
*Gretchen Weiners: Oh please. I hate my calves.*
*Regina George: At least you guys can wear halters. I've got man shoulders.*

**furgiveness**

What P.E.T.A. is going to deny you if you're ever caught in public wearing a real animal pelt.

**fuzzkill**

When you leave the house for a date in short-shorts or a skirt then realize
you totally missed a mound of hair on your knees while shaving and feel
insecure about it for the rest of the night.

# G

## gabbana boy

The retail equivalent of a cabana boy who brings you cocktails with little umbrellas and pretty things to try on while you're lounging at Neiman Marcus.

*Everyone knew Mrs. Howe was having an affair with the gabbana boy.*

## gallerinas

Those bright, young, pretty things who are both underpaid and overqualified to act as gatekeepers to the art world. They accept a pittance-paying job in exchange for all the hottest gossip and exposure at openings and auctions. And they're always the first to know when a designer like Marc Jacobs will be collaborating with an artist like Takashi Murakami.

## gallianos

Designer years (like dog years, but much shorter and used to measure the life span of a trend or a fruit fly).

## gaptimism

The belief that Gap is still cool, even though . . .

## garmed and dangerous

A phrase meaning "perfectly dressed in killer garments."

## gawkward

Mostly used to describe fledgling models who walk awkwardly down the runway as if they just had full-body casts removed. (It's like a car wreck—why can't we stop gawking at them?)

## getting waisted

Another term for "adding a belt."

## ghost hair

The newly severed long hair you keep reaching for as if it were still there, long after it's gone. Named for Demi Moore's crop in the movie *Ghost.*

## gilt trip

The sinking, remorseful feeling you get after purchasing too much on Gilt.

## glamdrogyny

Any display of glamour by a man that's so ostentatious it begs you to ask if he's actually a man. See: *Liberace*

# GLAMMIT!

## glammit!

An expression denoting frustration, often used by celebrities who get shafted on the red carpet the moment other, more glamorous celebrities show up and steal their thunder.

*"Glammit, Charlize Theron, you out-shined me again!" said everyone at the Oscars six years in a row.*

## glamour shots

Shot glasses full of potent alcohol meant for drinking when you spent hours getting ready and he doesn't even notice.

## glamputee

A person who somehow seems amputated without the signature accessories he or she has become well-known for (think Sally Jesse Raphael without her red glasses, Ellen DeGeneres without her sneakers, and Simon Doonan without his liberty florals).

## glammy

An enviably glam granny who's still got it.

## gloompaloompas

People who prefer to blend in on a dreary day by wearing head-to-toe black when a pop of color would really be so much more considerate of everyone around them.

## glossed and found

The designated place at a party (usually the kitchen sink) for misplaced cocktail glasses that have unidentified lipstick prints on them.

## glow job

Spray tan.

## glumbrella

An umbrella void of all color, pattern, or print.

## goat-scaping

Dressing vicariously through a pet or animal.

## goldilocks complex

When you can't quite get the right shade of blond, so you hop from salon to salon trying to get it just right.

## gosling bumps

The little baby goose bumps you get when anyone utters the words *Ryan Gosling* or *Bloomingdale's sale.*

## gorge

1. An abbreviation for gorgeous. 2. How to eat cake.

## gown syndrome

An unhealthy preoccupation with big white wedding dresses (symptoms include stockpiling bridal magazines and a sudden irrational desire to taste cake before breakfast).

*If left untreated, gown syndrome can cause a woman to choose the wrong husband.*

## grandma problems

To have grandma problems is to make sensible fashion and beauty choices, such as being in bed before midnight, wearing comfortable foot-wear, and appreciating what a good coral lipstick, a scarf, and an episode of *Murder, She Wrote* can do for you. See also: *grey hair, don't care*

**graphic t-shirt contest**

The street style equivalent of a wet T-shirt contest where two people compete to see whose graphic tee—and its message—can scream the loudest.

**gratisfaction**

The thrill of getting a gift with purchase you will actually use.

**grinade**

1. A smile bomb, dropped immediately after some intellectual wrongdoing has been committed in hopes beauty will prevail. 2. A tactic frequently used by contestants who make it to the Miss USA interview competition, embarrass themselves with a nonsensical answer, and advance to the next round anyway. See also: *Miss America's Most Wanted*

# H

## hack-in-the-box

Any cheap chain salon where hair-cutting techniques are learned from watching slasher films and stylists will break off most of your hair while violently combing through it.

## hairanoia

The fear that your favorite hairstylist will move or suffer a debilitating injury to the fingers.

## hair pollution

The signature trail of loose hairs you leave behind wherever you go, especially in your brush, in your car, on your bathroom floor, down the shower drain, and in your boyfriend's cereal dish.

## hairvoyant

How to describe a stylist with the ability to know exactly what you want without having to bring in pictures from magazines.

## hanger management

A special course to help budding Baby Janes acquire the skills needed to control their tempers in the presence of wire hangers. (Who doesn't love a good *Mommie Dearest* reference?)

## hasta la *ista*

Roughly translated as "goodbye *ista* words and good riddance." The suffix *ista* is the ultimate crime against nomenclature and is frequently added to any word to denounce one an expert (e.g., *fashionista*).

## hate affair

1. What happens when a well-dressed, perfectly sweet person becomes generally intolerable to other women for no explainable reason, even though she's not the least bit cruel, unattractive, or bimbo-like.
2. A full-fledged jealousy crush.

*Jill was sent to peer counseling for having torrid hate affairs with all the best-dressed girls in high school.*

## heirhead (pronounced "airhead")

A woman famed for only dating men who will inherit some kind of Greek shipping or Toaster Strudel fortune. See: *Hilton, Paris*

## hemetary

Where last season's micromini skirts are put to rest.

## hem-ocracy

The phenomenon by which every woman has a different idea of what constitutes a short skirt and therefore should technically be allowed to wear whatever she wants without scorn or derision from others. It is, after all, a free country.

**hemphasis**

Strategic use of a hemline to play up your best assets, be it ankles, knees, or thighs.

### hollisisters

A veritable girl band of adolescent teens bonded by a love of Hollister hoodies, rugby polos, and shirtless male models. Also known as *Abercronies,* depending on where they do most of their shopping.

## homage

A fancy way of saying something is inspired by something else, or more accurately, a total ripoff.

## honesty

All a girl can ask for from her bathroom mirror.

## hourglass

A borderline backhanded term often used to describe a woman's body, as if to suggest time is running out and she may not look like that forever.

## huelogy

The obituary-like announcement fashion magazines run to let you know which color has passed and which one will take its place this season.

## hunchback

The rounded shoulders and concave posture that can result from carrying a ridiculously heavy bag around every day for the rest of your life. Consider this a public service announcement.

## hungry

1. What fashion girls become when they are hunting for a job, a boyfriend, or an apartment in New York. 2. The opposite of healthy and the reason underweight models are banned in Israel. How do you say "More pie, please" in Israeli? See also: *NAGL*

# ON WEDNESDAYS WE WEAR PINK

**huemiliation**

Embarrassment caused by wearing the wrong color at the wrong time.

## huephoria

That euphoric feeling you get when you wear a bright, mood-lifting color and people comment on how fabulous it looks on you all day long.

## hunting for compliments

Like fishing for compliments, except the other person verbally holds a gun to your head and says, "How do I look?"

## human jeanome project

Denim cloning with the primary goal of coding pairs of jeans so that every size looks and fits the same, every time, ultimately preventing you from spending hours trying on every pair in the store because no two are alike. The *human jeanome* will also prevent manufacturers from using those annoying little stickers declaring a garment's flaws "one of a kind."

## husband (gay)

A gay husband is a fashion girl's best friend and/or soul-brain and quite possibly the only husband worth having.

## hydration

Starbucks run.

## hyper critical

What you become if you don't have a gay husband to remind you how freaking fabulous you are even though you walked all the way down Fifth Avenue with your skirt stuck in your ass today.

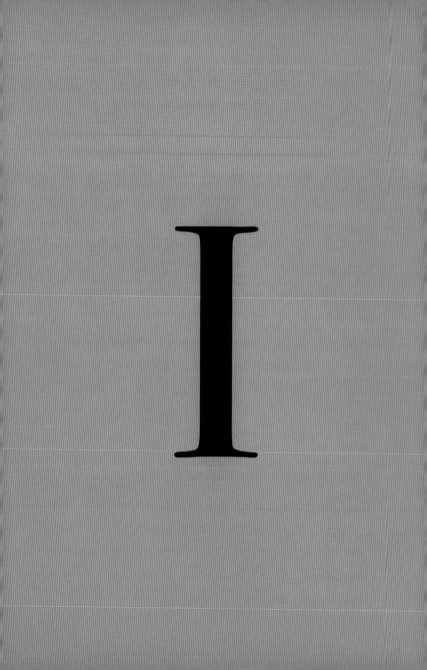

### ice rink

A gobstopper-sized diamond ring you could seriously skate on.

*"Did you see the ice rink on Colleen's ring finger? Her fiancé must be filthy rich."*

### idol blog worship

Religious-like devotion to fashion information not distributed by a glossy magazine.

### immaculate complexion

What every serum-loving gal aspires to: perfect skin in every light.

### IMMT

**I m**iss **m**y **t**an.

### immobility

A result of wearing 5" heels. See also: *Zaralysis*

# IDEAL BODY WEIGHT: BRADLEY COOPER ON TOP OF YOU.

**ideal body weight**

What some women spend eternity trying to achieve.

**indoorsy**

The polar opposite of outdoorsy.

*Indoorsy girls prefer not to go camping or be in direct sunlight for prolonged periods.*

**inner style compass**

Something Dorothy had in her all along; the ability to make the unexpected gingham and sequins work for her.

**inshopnia**

The inability to sleep after buying something so expensive you're ridden with the kind of guilt that you thought could only come from a one-night stand.

**instagramma**

A female who uses Instagram beyond the age of forty-five.

**intern 15**

The inevitable fifteen pounds lost during the first year of working at a fashion magazine due to a sudden *thinferiority complex* developed from being surrounded by size twos. Derived from the term *freshman 15*.

**irritable bowl syndrome**

A condition that strikes when, in the presence of strangers, your mom whips out childhood photos of you with your awful bowl haircut. Thanks, Mom.

**ironing deficiency**

A condition suffered by men who don't iron their shirts before leaving the house.

**is everything**

Something so fabulous the entire universe should revolve around it.

***ista* sunday**

The third Sunday in the paschal lunar month for celebrating *istas* in their various forms (including the *ista* bunny, who loves karats, obvi).

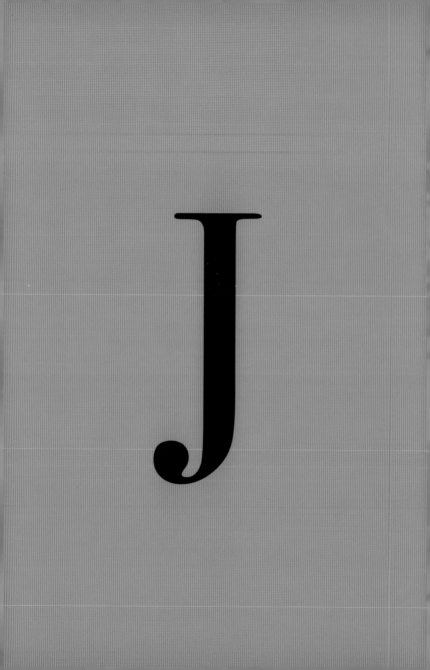

### jackie o-verkill

Any look that aggressively channels Jackie Onassis
(think oversized sunglasses, skirt suits, and sailor stripes).

### jack squats

Exercises that yield no visible results in time for swimsuit season.

### jet jaded

What a jet-setter becomes when he or she has traveled extensively and seen it all.

### jelirious

Deliriously jealous to the point of insanity.

### jenneration

A generation raised on *Keeping Up with the Kardashian* reruns. Everything we need to know about being women we learned from Bruce Jenner.

### jizzaster

1. What happens when your favorite dress acquires stains that are too embarrassing to bring to the dry cleaner *à la* Monica Lewinksy. 2. The official word for what Cameron Diaz's character's hair endured in *There's Something About Mary*.

### jolie de vivre

The elation you feel when a total stranger tells you that you resemble Angelina Jolie and that your cheekbones are "on point."

### jurassic parka

A large, archaic jacket from primitive times that no longer fits or is no longer in style, probably excavated from storage.

K

### ka-bloom!

The sound an obnoxiously loud floral pattern makes when it walks into a room.

### kardonkadonk

An extremely curvaceous female behind, exaggerated by a small waist, short physique, and bodycon dress (named for Kim Kardashian's *badonkadonk*).

### kate moss-achist

A person who derives both pleasure and pain from staring at, and comparing herself to, airbrushed pictures of Kate Moss.

### kiss and sell

Divulging the details of a scandalous affair to the tabloids for shoe money.

*Tiger should have known his mistresses were the kiss-and-sell type.*

## knit-picker

A friend who becomes overly fastidious about your appearance, causing her to pick lint off your sweater, call attention to the poppy seeds in your teeth, or tuck in your tags as though she were your mother.

## kors d'oeuvres

1. Accessories strategically placed at the front of a boutique to whet your spending appetite (named for all of the pretty little distractions on display at Michael Kors). 2. The least nourishing of the four fashion food groups. A department store is the only place where you are guaranteed to get a proper serving of all four groups: accessories, shoes, clothing, and bags.

*On a budget? Skip the Kors d'oeuvres and save room for the main course: a new dress.*

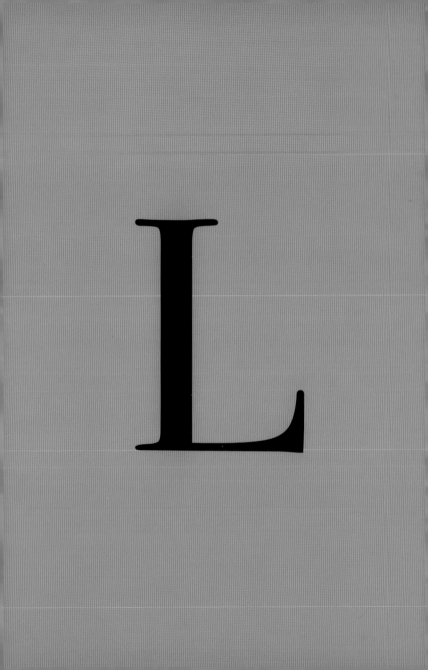

## label laundering

The act of removing a clothing label of little value and replacing it with a more expensive one so it looks like your outfit actually cost a fortune.

## lacoste intolerance

1. Much like lactose intolerance, Lacoste intolerance is an aversion to all things Lacoste. 2. A physical reaction (allergy) to anything too yuppy or preppy.

*People with Lacoste intolerance should steer clear of the Marina.*

## lacoste per wear

A mathematical equation that can be used to justify expensive purchases with tiny alligators on them.

## lacquer cabinet

Where you stash all your 80-proof nail polish.

*Let's meet up at my place tonight, raid the lacquer cabinet, and paint our nails before heading out to the bars.*

**larger than lagerfeld**

1. Used to describe something that is the next big thing. 2. Any trend so ginormously popular it's bigger than formerly overweight designer Karl Lagerfeld.

## lashturbation

The act of stimulating tiny, limp lashes with an oscillating, battery-powered mascara wand.

## left-breasted

What you are if your left breast is slightly better than your right. A person may also be considered *right-breasted*.

## legs for weeks

Weeks being infinitely longer than days (derived from the expression *legs for days*).

## lipochondria

The persistent, neurotic conviction that you have cellulite and need liposuction, even though nobody else sees it.

## lip tease

The cosmetic equivalent of a strip tease in which you apply lipstick in a seductive manner.

## little brown barf bag

An expression used by Bloomingdale's sales staff when random acquaintances ask if they can use their employee discount.

*Pass the little brown barf bag.*

## liquid courage

Skin confidence temporarily bestowed by the right foundation and totally destroyed by the wrong lighting.

## lobby-to-limo shoes

Non-functioning high heels that look really amazing but can't be worn more than a few steps without causing pain and a lifetime of podiatrist bills.

## lohab

Another name for the ultra-chic drug and alcohol rehabilitation services rendered at Promises LA and vital to over-partied starlets like Lindsay Lohan.

## lorena bobbitry

Impulsively cutting off one's own hair in a fit of rage, usually after a breakup or being repeatedly misunderstood by the automated telephone operator at Macy's.

## loubouti call

A spontaneous, no-strings shoe romp initiated by a last-minute phone call from a salesperson in the hopes you'll attend today's sale and buy new shoes (a.k.a. *sex-in-a-box*).

## louis vuittontourage

A group of gal pals carrying the exact same must-have handbag.

## LSD

Stands for **l**ittle **s**equin **d**ress or any dress that appears to be on hallucinogenic drugs.

## lust fund

A secret savings account that exists with the hope one day you'll be able to buy the one thing you want more than longer eyelashes.

# M

### magna klum laude

What's written on the diploma of every *Project Runway* alum who makes it into the final three. Named for supermodel host Heidi Klum.

### makeuppers

Cosmetics you buy with no real purpose other than to temporarily make yourself feel better on a bad day. See also: *Narscotics*

### makeup sponge

The beauty mooch who wants to know what makeup you use, where you got it, and how you get your eye shadow to look like that.

### mallzheizer's

A condition that causes you to forget where you parked at the mall.

### mane slaughter

Another way of saying "botched haircut" with jagged ends that look like they were cut with gardening shears.

**mane-ipulation**

The mind games your hair plays, causing it to behave the minute you
make an appointment to get it cut. (It's like it just knows.)

## mani-pause

The manicure equivalent of menopause where you reach a certain mature age and suddenly (and permanently) stop going to the nail salon because you realize how much money it will save you in the long run.

## marathon eating pants

Anything with an elastic waistband.

## mascarathon

What happens when your waterproof mascara won't come off, even with the strongest makeup remover.

## mastercardio

Exercising your credit card, which really doesn't feel like exercise at all. How very French.

## mattemoiselle

A nickname for oily-skinned women who spend their whole lives running from the grease police and never leave the house without blotting papers and shine-control powder.

## mayan shopocalypse

A hoax instigated by retail marketers who want you to shop like there's no tomorrow.

## MEH

"**My e**yelashes **h**urt," said after a long night of swilling too much free champagne and waking up so tired you can barely lift a lash.

*Do I really have to go to work today? MEH!*

### mirror thirty

A scant thirty-minute window of time when the natural light is the most flattering and you look your best in photos (around 4 p.m.).

### miss america's most wanted

A soon-to-air show hosted by John Walsh that focuses on how to protect your family and local community from criminally fake boobs, big hair, and nonsensical on-stage interviews.

### missing parsons report

Official paperwork documenting the release of your favorite *Project Runway* contestant (likely never to be seen on television again) from Parsons School of Design.

### missile toe

Dangerously pointy shoes resembling war missiles.

### mist connection

What's happening when you catch a whiff of a great-smelling stranger who must have walked through a mist of expensive cologne this morning and your nose now feels the need to follow him all over town.

## MOD

**M**odel **o**ff **d**uty.

**moda operandi**

Personal style strategy.

**mug burn**

Skin irritation caused by making out with a bearded boy, also known as *crush rash*.

**multiple purse-onality disorder**

A condition marked by the unexplainable need to own a different purse for every mood, occasion, and whim.

**must-have-alance**

What happens when you open the door to your closet and all the things you wanted so badly but never wear come tumbling out like a natural disaster. See also: *shoe-nami*

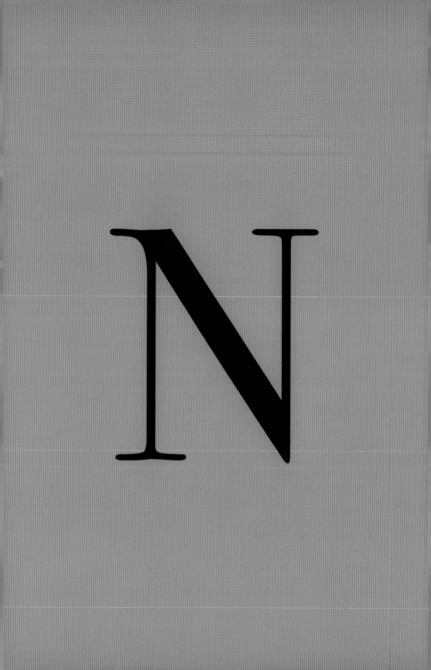

## NAGL

**N**ot **a g**ood **l**ook.

## narc jacobs

A person who calls you out for wearing a designer knock-off in front of other people who never would have known the difference.

*Now everybody at work knows my bag's fake. Thanks a lot, Narc Jacobs!*

## narscolepsy

Falling asleep in your favorite Nars makeup without washing your face.

## narscotics

Any Nars makeup so amazing it causes an addiction akin to cocaine.

*Orgasm Blush is my Narscotic of choice.*

## nastyplasty

Botched plastic surgery.

## natch

An abbreviation for natural or the "no-makeup look," which actually takes hours to achieve and many washcloths to wash off. See: *Hudson, Kate*

## near-debt experience

Barney's New York, third floor.

## near-deaf experience

What happens when you step into an Abercrombie & Fitch without the requisite ear plugs. (You may also need a gas mask and flashlight to navigate the store.)

## neckognize

To recognize a woman's true age by the rings around her neck, despite her countless facial lifts and hours logged at the gym. You can prevent people from *neckognizing* that you just turned fifty by wearing scarves and never taking them off.

## neet freak

Someone who is fastidious about depilating her private parts with Neet or Nair, even when nobody else will see.

## newlywedhead

The un-fussiest of hairstyles you rock on return from your honeymoon after rolling around in bed together for seven days straight.

## newmonia

An epidemic causing clothes to lose their luster after the first time you wear them.

## new year's heave

A national holiday when dateless women everywhere clean their closets to make room for new clothes in the new year.

## ninety-nine (blogger) problems

A phrase that means "a lot of problems" but, specifically, nothing to wear will never be one.

## nomshell

The gorgeous, slender, envy-eliciting model who takes you by surprise by wolfing down not only her meal, but also yours, with the weight going straight to her boobs every time.

## nosetalgia

Wistful affection for a star's schnoz, pre-surgery.

*Whenever I watch the earliest* Friends *reruns, I get nosetalgic for Jen's old nose.*

## nothing-to-wear stare

What happens every time you stand in front of your closet with your mouth gaping open, not knowing what to wear.

**notorious b-a-g**

Any purse that's achieved notoriety for its ability to feed a small village
with its ridiculous price tag.

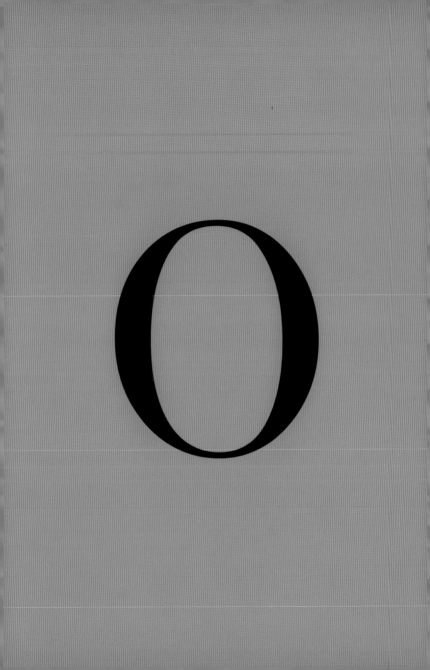

## obsessive-compulsive dior-der

The uncontrollable impulse to hoard Dior lipsticks in every color.

*It wasn't until I saw Liz's makeup bag that I realized she may have Obsessive-Compulsive Dior-der.*

## obsessorize

To obsess over which accessories you'll wear with something that's particularly difficult to style, like chambray.

## obsessive pore disorder

The compulsive need to pick, prod, or pinch pores in front of a magnifying mirror when under stress.

## off the rack

An expression used to describe something newly purchased and fabulous, derived from the expression *off the hook.*

## old schoul

Vintage Proenza Schouler.

## olsenility

The process of aging before your time because of very mature wardrobe choices, a term named for the Olsen twins and their elder-fied red carpet styling decisions.

## on-trend

A very official way of saying something's in style, having a moment, and about to be obsolete in six months.

## OPP

**O**ther **p**eople's **P**rada.

## OTT

**O**ver **t**he **t**op or *thisclose* to being off the deep end.

## overalls to the wall

To push fashion boundaries by rocking something fashionably heinous, like denim overalls.

*We're going out tonight, overalls to the wall.*

## over the hilfiger

The age at which it becomes inappropriate to dress like you're a collegiate from Nantucket. Named for Tommy Hilfiger's collections and the term "over the hills."

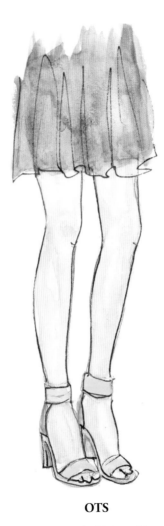

### OTS

**O**pen **t**oe **s**eason, the most wonderful time of the year if you can afford
bi-weekly pedicures.

# P

**'pagne** (pronounced "pain")

A throbbing headache caused by swilling too much complimentary champagne while waiting forever for a fashion show to start

*The 'pagne is doing me in; I have to eat something, anything, right now!*

## panis attack

Panic at the sight of your own *panis* (panis being the very official medical term for muffin top).

## pantsdemic

Widespread illness happening below the waist, all over town, in the form of hideous pants.

*This harem pantsdemic needs to stop before someone trips and falls on their own drop-crotch.*

## pantyoxidant

Special wash that keeps delicate unmentionables looking young forever.

## pathological buyer

Someone who engages in covert shopping missions, keeping them a secret from her husband by destroying all evidence or having bills sent to an alternate address.

## peplumps

Phantom curves created by wearing flared peplum.

## pepto-abysmal

The ugliest-ever shade of pink resembling a bottle of Pepto Bismol.

## perflector

Any reflective surface other than a mirror used to fix your appearance, like a store or car window.

**perfuffle**

A sudden disturbance of nasal passageways caused by someone wearing
too much perfume.

### perfume curfew

An early curfew that your parents will most definitely enforce if you leave wearing too much perfume while you still live under their roof. Never tell them you're going to an all-girl sleepover then blow your cover by wearing Daisy Marc Jacobs.

*Always put fragrance on after leaving the house to keep your parents from enforcing a strict perfume curfew.*

**persnippety**

A term used to describe a very fussy, argumentative hairstylist who thinks he or she knows best.

**pervacateur**

The creepy guy who accompanies his girlfriend shopping at Agent Provacateur, all the while getting turned on by eyeing the skimpy little lace things you're about to try on.

**piles**

A condition wherein you become too busy, tired, or lazy to do laundry and are forced to wear whatever's clean—or, in some extreme cases, whatever's been lying around in the hamper.

*Jenna's all wrinkly again; that girl's got chronic piles.*

**PHI**

**P**ositive **h**eel **i**nclination, or the height of your heels compared to standing on a steep hill.

**phonytail**

A fake ponytail purchased from a mall kiosk.

### photosensitivity

Contrary to the official Merriam-Webster definition, photosensitivity is not an abnormally high sensitivity to sunlight, at least not when it pertains to fashion girls. It's actually the sensitivity to having anyone take your photo when you feel you don't look your best.

### plane jane

The official name for the "civilian" no-makeup look that celebrities probably spend at least two hours trying to achieve because they want to appear effortless and relatable while being photographed walking through the terminal at JFK International or LAX.

### platinumb

The feeling of being so over-shopped that your Platinum card has lost that loving feeling.

*Never thought I'd say it, but I've finally gone platinumb.*

### pleather weather

A perfectly windy 60 degrees that promises to keep sweat at bay and prevents pleather from sticking to the skin.

### plus-onesie

Bringing a baby to the social event of the season because you can't find a sitter.

### PMS

**P**retty **m**ean **s**alesperson.

**porecast**

A daily weather assessment that helps you determine which moisturizer to wear.

*Today's porecast is perfectly sunny, which calls for a lightweight, oil-free formula with SPF 50+.*

**porensic evidence**

Skin damage that can only be seen under a specialized light at the SK-II skincare counter.

**poregasm**

What you experience when a painful zit finally comes to a head and the extraction results in instant relief.

**porter geist** (pronounced "por-tay" meaning "to wear" in French)

Something hideous you wore in the past that still haunts you in photos to this day.

**poshture**

A special way of standing up straight that makes you instantly appear more regal and slender, named for Victoria Posh Beckham.

**postparty depression**

A type of clinical depression that affects some guests after a really great fashion party is over. Feelings of loss and sadness are worsened by the emergence of undereye circles and dehydrated skin from drinking too much.

## post-traumatic tress

An anxiety disorder that develops after getting a horrible haircut and causes you to never trust another stylist again.

## prayers

"Please grant me serenity and a really awesomely distressed leather jacket." Usually directed toward All Saints, and the St. Regis spa on East 55th Street.

## preen estate

Prime bathroom counter real estate, which no living quarters should be without.

## prepsicle

A die-hard preppy who prefers to wear her sweater tied around her shoulders, rather than on her back, even though it's freezing outside.

## pretty party

The new pity party.

*I'm hosting the pretty party of the season! BYOB (bring your own Botox).*

## primcess

A woman who wears all things elegant and ladylike. See: *Middleton, Kate*

## primperazzi

Cosmetics sales people who lunge at you and follow you around the store asking if you want a makeover as though you desperately need one.

## prisoner of wardrobe

What you become when you turn down an invitation because you have nothing to wear even though your closet begs to differ.

*I regret to inform you that I can't come to your party; I'm a prisoner of wardrobe.*

## promocide

A shopping crime wherein a special offer or promotion is left to die without being taken advantage of. A mortal sin.

## promosexual

Someone aroused by sales, discounts, and exclusive in-store offers.

## purge-gatory

The special hell that is needing something desperately after you've thrown it away in a mass closet exodus.

## PUI

Stands for **p**lucking **u**nder the **i**nfluence. See: *bad idea*

**pursefolio**

An extensive collection of financial investments worn on the arm.

## pursepiration

Beads of sweat that accumulate from carrying your house on your back all day.

## p-whipped

A person whose wardrobe is dominated by Prada.

*Another Saffiano Lux Tote? You are so P-whipped.*

## PYT

Stands for **p**retty **y**um **t**hing, a derivative of yummy, which also means coveted, craved, or "so cute I could eat it up."

### quack face

An extreme form of *duck face* (achieved by sucking in the cheeks and pouting the lips), abused by someone to the point of looking insane or "quacked out."

R

**recessionitis**

Pain in the wrists caused by repeatedly scrolling on Pinterest to keep yourself from shopping during a recession.

**regret-me-nots**

The handbags, shoes, and accessories you buy with the intention of loving them forever because they'll never make you feel as though you shouldn't have had that last piece of lemon poppy seed cake.

**restless leggings syndrome**

That feeling you get after you buy new clothes and suddenly need to make plans to hit the town, just so you can wear them.

**retailgating**

Throwing a parking lot party outside a store before it opens, complete with a portable grill and watermelon wine coolers.

## retailsuscitation

When a day of shopping brings you back to life after you've been feeling stressed or depressed.

## re-tale therapy

The act of recounting your shopping tales so that anyone who could not accompany you can live vicariously through them.

## retin-AWOL

A sudden absence from one's usual social scene due to the overuse of flesh-eating Retin-A.

## returning spree

What follows a very impulsive shopping spree.

## reynold's wrap

Another name for the clingy dresses worn by Blake Lively that simultaneously reveal lots of cleavage and lots of thigh, contrary to fashion advice to choose one to avoid looking like a hooker. Named for Ryan Reynolds, the leading man Lively snagged with said garments.

## rich girl hair

The most privileged hair in the world, exposed only to the finest products and Evian water and treated like rare silk since birth. See: *Palermo, Olivia*

### riding one's pigtails

What happens when older women in the fashion workplace steal the ideas of younger women with their fingers on the pulse of pop culture. Derived from the term *riding one's coattails.*

### riet

A type of crash diet that takes place before a reunion, which causes severe crankiness and inevitably a riot in your household.

### robert dinero

A term of endearment for any man whose manner of dress reeks of wealth or *mucho dinero,* usually evidenced by his choice of watch, shoes, or wallet.

### rosemary's baby bump

A fleeting stomach bump caused when something evil possesses you to scarf a very large meal, followed by dessert, two more helpings, and copious amounts of booze, causing everyone around you to wonder if you're pregnant.

### russell crowe's feet

The lines around an older man's eyes, which unfairly make him look distinguished and rugged.

### ruthless disappointment

Nate Berkus for Target and any other designer collaboration from which we'll never recover.

### rush hour roulette

The gamble you take when you oversleep after staying out too late and have to do your makeup in the car or on the subway on the way to work without much control over the outcome. Living on winged eyeliner and a prayer.

S

**sackreligious**

How to describe a person who worships at the altar of the latest It bag.

**sackrifice**

What you endure when you choose a clutch that won't fit more than a credit card, phone, and lipstick, forcing you to leave everything else you need at home or stuff it in your bra.

**salon chairapy**

The phenomenon in which you're compelled to spill all sorts of intimate details you would never tell anyone else in your stylist's chair, also known as *trimtimacy*.

**salve-vation**

Relief from dry lips bestowed by some form of balm or salve.

## sartorial dysfunction

A form of *twincest* wherein two people dress alike or sport the same hairstyle, making it impossible for the rest of the world to decipher who is who.

*Remember when Katie Holmes turned into Victoria Beckham? Or when Brad Pitt and Jennifer Aniston sported the same highlights? Hello, sartorial dysfunction.*

## sascrotch

An overgrown bikini line *à la Harry and the Hendersons.*

## scarfings

An incriminating kind of crumb commonly found in the Hermès scarves of fashion girls whose offices are directly across the street from a bakery. Scarfings tend to be pastel-colored and serve as evidence that you just ran across the street to stuff your face with macarons when you were supposed to be in a meeting.

## scentimental

What you become for a fleeting moment when you catch a whiff of a former boyfriend's cologne on someone else or smell a favorite perfume from your past.

*I got so scentimental last night, I just curled up in the fetal position and listened to love songs from the '80s.*

## score

To get something for at least 50 percent off the retail price.

## selfie-affirmation

A sense of self-worth derived from taking your own picture with a camera phone while wearing new clothes.

## selfie-destructive

A term used to describe a celebrity who tweets hot mess pictures of herself then wakes up to thousands more concerned/fascinated followers the next day, also known as *selfie-mutilation* or *selfie-sabotage*. See: *Bynes, Amanda*

## selftantrum

The shrieking freak-out that ensues when you wake up with orange palms and streaked legs the day of a pool party.

## sensible

Boring.

## sephoradisiac

A means of getting in the mood right before you go on a big date by buying new beauty products, spraying yourself with sensual fragrance, or having your makeup done at Sephora.

## september issues

The official name for the citywide stress that goes on in September during New York Fashion Week.

*Don't even talk to me right now, I've got serious September issues.*

## sequins

At breakfast. In broad daylight. Bravo.

## serendipretty

1. When a good skin day and good hair day coincide. 2. When a last-minute invitation strikes when you are without a makeup bag but happen to be near a department store to touch up your makeup.

## serial monogrammy

Devotion to one type of logo-splattered clothing from head to toe.

## ser*ummmm*

Named for very expensive skincare that *ummmmm,* after four weeks, still does not appear to be reducing the appearance of anything.

## sewbrity test

What you should give yourself before attempting to operate a sewing machine after a few margaritas.

## sexfoliation

The process of taking a loofah, pumice stone, or coarse apricot kernal scrub to every nook and cranny of your body in anticipation of having sex.

## sex pack abs

Chiseled, come-hither abdominals, best accentuated with a teeny weeny bikini.

## sextile

Any sensuous textile that says "take me to bed" or is worn for the purpose of seduction, such as silk, satin, or cashmere.

## shelf-ish

How to describe your closet-hogging husband or roommate.

## shop tease

When a store has what you want in stock, but your size is occupied by the mannequin and they won't let you rip it off of her.

## shoeffeur

Another term for cab drivers, the unsung heroes who save millions of urban women from hobbling down the street on their aching feet every day.

*A lady always generously tips her shoeffeur.*

## shoenami

What would happen if an innocent bystander were to open the door to your closet, forcing him to hit high ground quickly.

## shoenicorn

A fabled shoe of legendary proportions, like Manolo Blahnik Campari Mary Janes.

## shoevenir

Shoes bought for the sole purpose of remembering a vacation.

## shopboparazzi

The banner ads that follow your every click after you've been shopping on a site like Shop Bop.

## shopper's block

A mental state akin to writer's block during which you cannot find anything you like or want to buy.

## shopping casket

The wooden box your husband will bury you in when he finds out about your new seven-hundred-dollar dress.

## shopping stand-in

The friend you should always bring shopping so she can stand in line as a placeholder while you continue to scour the racks.

## shoppy hour

The new happy hour.

## shornacopia

1. Total body hairless bliss. 2. A feeling that only lasts for a few days or until the stubble grows back.

## shrekitude

A fugly, hot mess that's beyond *drekitude*.

## signature walk

The official name for a model's runway presence. If she happens to walk like a gimp, calling it a signature walk makes it fierce.

## singerie

Particularly sinful underpinnings created for the sole purpose of getting nasty.

## skinny hat

A hat created with the sole intention of making people feel bad about their head size.

## skinsanity

A form of self-sabotage that takes place in front of a magnifying mirror, causing you to pick, poke, and pinch otherwise invisible pores into inflamed oblivion, especially while drunk or hormonally enraged.

## skinspiracy

What's going on when celebrities withhold their beauty secrets from the rest of womankind and act like all they use is a bar of drugstore soap when they really use an exotic five-thousand-dollar cream.

## skinsomnia

The unfortunate effects of not getting enough beauty sleep, including chronic dull face. See also: *vitamin Z deficiency*

### skintuition

That gut feeling that tells you a zit is coming on before it's even surfaced.

*My skintuition tells me it must be that time of the month.*

### skirting

The act of flirting from across a crowded room simply by working a flashy little skirt.

### skurvy

Skinny with curves. See: *Swanepoel, Candice*

### slanket

A loose dress resembling a blanket with sleeves, sometimes with pockets that are perfect for stashing appetizers at parties.

### socially transmitted debt (STD)

What you get for trying to keep up with the Kardashians.

### SOL

Stands for **s**orry **o**ut of **l**ipstick, or what to say when someone who's getting over a cold wants to share your Juicy Tube.

### spandex-hibitionism

A perversion in which a person enjoys the indecent exposure of every lump and bump on his or her body and chooses to flaunt it in Spandex.

## spanxgiving

The day after Thanksgiving when women who ate too much give thanks for the invention of the blessed body-shaper Spanx.

*When you're a good cook, every day is Spanxgiving.*

## spanx-iety

The fear that a date will discover your shapewear under your dress.

## spare the hair day

The one day per month you should be forgoing blow-drying, heated styling tools, and product pollution to give damaged hair a rest.

## spoof-offs

The new knock-off labels: Féline, Homiés, Hotmés.

## stare-anoia

The self-conscious assumption that someone is staring because there's something wrong with you when really it's because you look *amaze-za-za-zing*.

## stilecho

The echo of stilettos on linoleum tile.

## stilt-letto

Any stiletto so tall walking in it qualifies you for a job as a stilt walker at the circus.

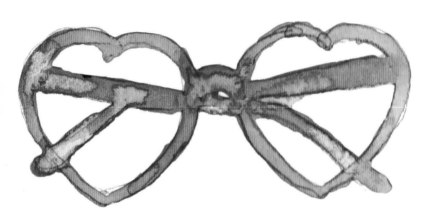

### specshibitionist

A person who makes wildly obnoxious glasses the focal point of his
or her look. See: *John, Elton*

### stompquake

When a stampede of models come charging down the runway stomping to the death.

### store-igami

The art of folding paper receipts into decorative figurines.

### storenication

Sex in a fitting room.

### store-o-scopes

A sophisticated new marketing strategy that enables retailers to know exactly what you're likely to buy based on your astrological sign.

### storeplay

When boutiques try to get you all excited and in the mood by sending you emails about a sale days before it happens.

### straydar

The sensory radar built into your forefinger that detects any stray chin hairs you may have missed in the magnifying mirror.

### street currency

The value of an outfit on the street, as measured by its photogenic capabilities.

**stripe tease**

The fashion equivalent of a Jedi mind trick in which a woman wears
stripes to make herself appear smaller than she really is. (Horizontal
stripes should always be avoided for this purpose.)

### stress aging

When some kind of trauma (i.e., awkwardly coming face-to-face with a legend like Nina Garcia in the hallway at work) causes you wrinkles, grey hair, and irritable bowels before your time. Hello Activia.

### stressalyzer

A measure of stress, indicated by the sweat stains under the arms of a silk blouse.

### success-ories

Expensive-looking accessories that give the impression of wealth and success and should be worn when you want a promotion.

### sunbrero

An enormous wide-brim hat donned for no other reason than you want to have the prettiest skin when you're an old lady in the nursing home.

### super bowl bumday

The one day when you can go shopping in sweatpants and no makeup because everyone you know is at home watching the game.

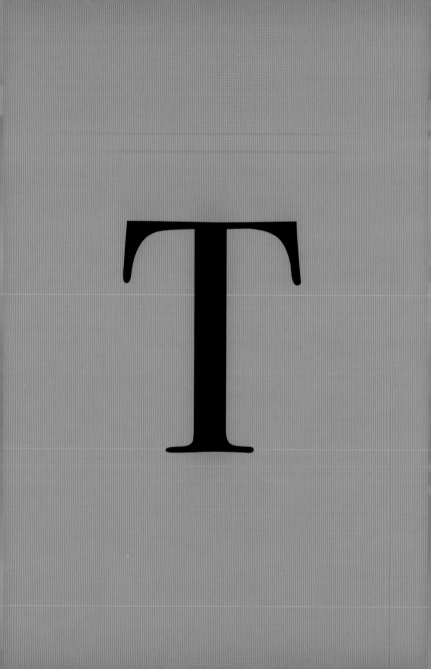

**tagony**

When the tag inside your clothes itches so bad it drives you to crazy extremes, like yanking it off with your teeth or going topless.

**tanesthesia**

Tanning to numb your problems.

**tanarchy**

Rebelling against mainstream ideals of beauty with ultra-pale, ultra-healthy, ultra-flawless skin, also known as *tan repelling*. Seriously, someone needs to start a Tan Repeller blog.

**tank toppings**

Accessories, the proverbial sprinkles on an otherwise basic vanilla tank top.

*Somebody please stop me from oinking out on tank toppings at Forever 21.*

## TDF

**To die for**, which is slightly more coveted than whatever you're willing to kill for.

## teapot-itis

A condition causing young girls to strike a little teapot pose (arm on the hip, chin down, eyes up) in the presence of a camera.

## terminal chillness

An affliction suffered by top models whose height and glassy stare make eye contact impossible.

## textual harassment

When an aggressive salesperson gets hold of your number and starts texting you about upcoming sales and promotions without your permission, also known as *textploitation*.

## thong-distance

A type of long-distance relationship that manages to last a lot longer than anyone thought possible because of sexy lingerie pictures exchanged via text.

*I'm in a thong-distance relationship with Derek Jeter. The problem is, so are hundreds of other women.*

## thong antlers

The waistband of a thong, which btw should never protrude from the top of low rise jeans. Because thong antlers are wildly inappropriate, some women resort to not wearing any underwear and instead flash plumber's crack atop their barstool.

**titastrophe**

What happens when your boobs escape confinement.

**thick skin**

The ultimate must-have if you want to be a model, acquired through years of criticism about the way you look.

**titunic**

A shapeless, oversized tunic that makes you resemble a large, sinking ship.

**totes**

1. Handbags with parallel handles. 2. An abbreviation for totally.

**the tourettes set**

Cuckoo people who yell out what they think of your new hairstyle ("You cut your hair! I liked it better before!"), never mind the fact that you didn't ask for their opinion.

**tragical**

Something so tragic, it's magical.

**trample sale**

A showcase of designer steals where the risk of getting trampled by other shoppers is high.

**tranny-mosity**

A state of anger and animosity on those off days when you feel like Jared Leto makes a better looking woman than you.

**trendorphins**

Hormones released by shopping and proven to produce the same pharmacological effects as Prozac.

**tress relief**

That shiny new feeling when you finally get your wildly overgrown hair trimmed and conditioned after depriving yourself for too long.

**trendship**

A fair weather relationship forged over material things that will likely be so over next season.

**trendwreck**

The fashion equivalent of a train wreck, and we all can't help but stare.

**tressticles**

A hairstyle resembling a large ballsack, worn on the tippy top of the head, also known as *scrot knot*.

*When did tressticles become en vogue? I can barely stop laughing.*

**t-rexia**

What happens when you squeeze into a t-shirt that's several sizes too tight, cutting off your circulation and causing your arms to become vestigial at your sides like a dinosaur.

**trimpathy**

Expressing sympathy and support after a girlfriend gets a bad haircut.

**trimpotence**

What happens to a hairstylist when he or she can't recreate the look you loved last time.

**tryphoon**

A disastrous mess of hangers and clothing left behind on a fitting room floor after someone else tried on multiple outfits in a whirlwind.

**tryrany**

When a salesperson keeps asking if you're ready for a fitting room so she can stuff you inside of it without actually helping you—and still get the commission.

**try-sexual**

A person who's willing to try on anything knowing it has a 50 percent chance of looking a lot better on her than it does on the hanger.

*I love shopping with Joanne; she really embraces her try-sexuality.*

**tryumph**

Victory in the fitting room, at last!

## tush-ups

Stealth bun-squeezing exercises, akin to kegels, that will improve the way you look in leggings if done repetitively during three-hour meetings.

## tweehab

An intensive form of rehabilitation for Twitter addicts who divulge way too many details about what they're doing or thinking throughout the day, and take way too many pictures of their haircuts. See also: *tw-ourettes*

*Refraining from Tweeting pictures of the breathtaking view from my room in Tweehab was the hardest part.*

## tweetox

A detox from Tweeting, usually a 24-hour period in which you refrain from logging into Twitter. People who tweet 3–10 times a day tend to undergo tweetox before checking themselves into tweehab.

## twelve-steps program

A course of action for women addicted to shoes that prohibit them from walking more than twelve steps in an evening.

## twerkout

Any workout involving a pole and requiring you to channel your inner stripper.

## two-comma coma

A result of seven-figure debt (e.g., $7,000,000).

**tw-ourettes**

The Twitter equivalent of Tourettes where you can't stop tweeting about what you just bought, what you just had for breakfast, and what you just overheard the people next to you saying.

**typothermia**

A condition that happens to fashion editors and writers who work in poorly ventilated cubicles: their well-manicured hands eventually turn a brilliant shade of cobalt blue, hence the invention of fingerless gloves for typing at a keyboard.

*Can someone turn up the heat? I'm about to get typothermia up in here.*

**tyrade**

The official name for the *America's Next Top Model* situation that happens every season where Tyra Banks goes ballistic on a contestant who's in the wrong place at the wrong time with the wrong attitude.

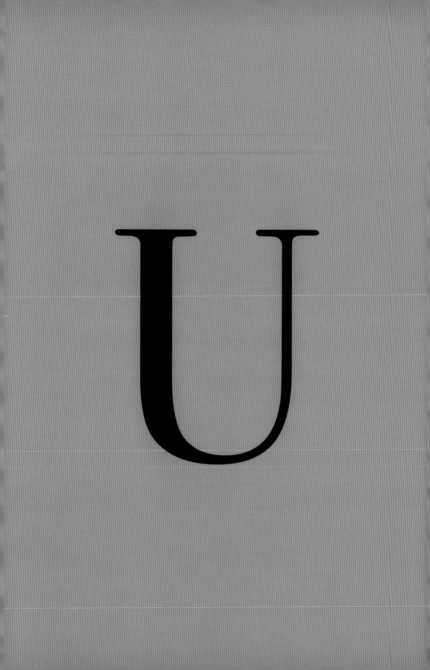

**uggasm**

Relief from slipping your foot into a marshmallow-like Ugg boot after wearing heels.

**ultra-mega-hyper-superficial**

Chronically shallow.

**underage dressing**

Dressing like jail bait over the age of forty.

**unitarded**

What you become when temporarily handicapped by a unitard you must step out of before going to the bathroom.

**urban fashion legend**

A style myth that circulates as truth.

*Don't believe those urban fashion legends; you can totally wear white after Labor Day and guys definitely make passes at girls wearing glasses.*

**vajaycay**

An all-girls vacation or road trip involving extensive shopping by day and looking for hot guys by night.

**valentino's day**

The day after Valentine's, an unofficial holiday for self-gifting created by fashionistas who got totally jipped by their boyfriends and will make it up to themselves by buying something scandalously expensive.

**vanity case**

What to call someone so obsessed with the way they look, they've become a total basket case (named for the carry-all that houses all your makeup).

*I liked Liz better before she moved to LA and became a total vanity case.*

**vanity plates**

Dinnerware that confirms your high-fashion status at parties.

## velvetween

A heinous material that's somewhere between crushed velvet and felt.

## very editorial

Another way of saying "don't attempt to wear this look in real life."

## VFL

Stands for **v**isible **f**oundation **l**ine, just as scandalous as visible panty line.

## vitamin z deficiency

A sore absence of beauty sleep or Zzzzs.

*I've been up for seventy-two hours straight; I worry I might develop a Vitamin Z deficiency.*

## vocationship

When you date someone at work because he's the only man in the accessories department.

## von furstenburglar

B*tch stole my wrap dress.

**walk-away rule**

A rule created to help you practice self-restraint while shopping.
It involves putting a desired item on hold, walking away from it for
twenty-four hours, and taking that time to mull over whether you really
need it. If it's true love, you'll still be thinking about it in the morning.

**wardrobe atrophy**

A loss of desire to dress up, usually caused by a sore absence of chic
(e.g., working at home or being surrounded by other people who never
dress up). See also: *Western casualization*

**was-girl**

A former It-girl.

*Correction to the article we ran in Page 6 last week: Dottie Kincaid is not a*
*has-been, she's a was-girl.*

**weardrobe**

The small portion of your wardrobe that you actually wear.

*Not to be confused with your wardrobe, your weardrobe accounts for a small
percentage of functioning clothes in your closet.*

## western casualization

The dressing down of Western civilization, propelled by laziness and the belief that dressing up suggests over-eagerness.

## whelmed

The balance between overwhelming and underwhelming.

*I was perfectly whelmed by Salma Hayek's Oscars dress.*

## whooshing

Airbrushing beyond recognition.

## whormones

Hormones that make you want to dress scantily on certain days of the month, as dictated by your body's ovulation cycle.

*Girl 1: Woah, what's with the micromini skirt?*
*Girl 2: What can I say? My whoremones are raging.*

## whornaments

Cheap-looking accessories.

## willpower

Never heard of it.

## window shopping

Again, never heard of it.

## wintour olympics

The ultimate test of stamina and strength requiring a fashion editor's assistant to jump through hoops all over town, despite sleet, snow, and gloom of night. Named for *Vogue* editrix Anna Wintour and her infamously evil ways.

*Poor Genevieve, I wonder if she'll make it through the Wintour Olympics or quit before the fall issue goes to print?*

## witherspooning

The act of letting a poor, unassuming one-night stand know he's in the presence of greatness. Or, specifically, the moment you wake up in a strange person's apartment, designer clothes strewn about, and say with a straight face, "You're about to find out who I am." Derived from Reese Witherspoon's disorderly run-in with a Georgia State Trooper.

## wobbly

Another term for can't walk in heels to save her life.

## wombshell

A pregnant bombshell who manages to look ravishing even though her womb has been stretched to the size of a watermelon. See: *Kerr, Miranda*

**work**

1. To show people how flipping fabulous you are (also spelled *w-e-r-k*).
2. What you do for free all summer after being hired as a fashion intern.

X

## XL bomb

What happens when a man buys you a sweater for Christmas and offensively overestimates your size.

*Nina: So what'd he get you for Christmas?*
*Gina: An XL bomb.*
*Nina: Ouch.*

## x-mas mourning

Another term for Christmas day, when you get a hideous item of clothing or jewelry you can't return because you'll have to wear it to spare someone's feelings.

Y

### yesters

So hopelessly twenty-four hours ago.

*Wide-leg trousers are yesters, but I'm sure they'll be back with a vengeance.*

### youthemism

Any euphemism that makes being older sound awesomely sophisticated (e.g., "a woman *d'un certain age*").

### yo-yo mode

Crash dieting for a big event with a fridge full of Yoplait.

*Get your cruel cookie jar out of here; I'm in yo-yo mode!*

Z

## zaralysis

A loss of significant movement (e.g., having to sit all night) due to cute but questionably made shoes under fifty dollars from a fast-fashion brand like Zara.

## z-cup

The largest boobs you wish you'd never seen in the women's locker room.

## zitzophrenia

Psycho skin with unpredictable hormonal breakouts.

## zborn-acne (pronounced Zpornak-ne)

A form of acne brought on by man-related stress. Inspired by Dorothy's ex-husband Stan Zbornak who would always show up unannounced and ruin her perfectly good mood on *Golden Girls*.

*Patient: Every time my ex rears his head, so do the pimples on my chin.*
*Dermatologist: Sounds like you've got Zborn-acne. They'll go away when he does.*

**zoedependency**

When celebrities become reliant on guidance from Rachel Zoe, rendering them incapable of landing on the best-dressed list without her.

# Sartorial gibberish

Fashion naming takes its cues from Gregor Mendel's principles of crossbreeding—the sounds and meanings of existing words are fused together to create totally new trends (most of them hard to wear or say with a straight face). According to the laws of nomenclature, if a skirt breeds with a pair of shorts, the off-spring will be a *skort*. Similarly, if a watch procreates with a bracelet, a *watchlet* is born.

**Blurt** blouse + skirt
**Coatigan** coat + cardigan
**Flatforms** flats + platforms
**Glamping** glamorous camping
**Glittens** gloves + mittens
**Glunge** glam + grunge
**Guyliner** man eyeliner
**Gypset** gypsy + jet set
**Hikini** hi-cut + bikini
**Jeggings** jeans + leggings
**Jombats** jeggings + combat pants
**Jorts** jeans + shorts
**Mangs** man bangs
**Mankini** man bikini

**Manorexia** man + model
**Manscara** man mascara
**Manties** man panties
**Meggings** man leggings
**Mube** maxi + tube dress
**Pleather** plastic + leather
**Shootie** shoe + bootie
**Skort** skirt + shorts
**Skouser** skirt + trouser
**Tee-jamas** t-shirt + pajama
**Treggings** trouser + leggings
**Watchlet** watch + bracelet
**Whorts** Winter + shorts
**Wootie** wedge + bootie

# Tongue-twisting fashion labels

Andrew Gn ("jen")

Anna Sui ("swee")

Anya Hindmarch ("ahn-ya hind-march")

Balenciaga ("ba-len-see-ah-ga")

Bagdley Mishchka ("badge-lee meesh-ka")

Balmain ("bal-mah")

Bebe ("bee-bee")

Behnaz Sarafpour ("ben-oz sah-rafpoor")

Bottega Veneta ("bo-teg-a ven-e-ta")

Bulgari ("bool-gah-ree")

Burberry Prorsum ("bur-bur-ree pror-some")

Ceasare Paciotti ("chay-sah-rah pah-chee-oh-tee")

Chaiken ("chay-ken")

Chanel ("shun-elle")

Christian Lacroix ("la-kwa")

Christian Louboutin ("loo-boo-tan")

Comme des Garcons ("comb day gar-sone")

Dolce Gabbana ("dole-chay gob-ah-na")

Dries Van Noten ("dreez van no-ten")

Ermenegildo Zegna ("er-men-a-geel-do zen-ya")

Etienne Aigner ("eh-tee-yeh on-yay")

Etro ("ay-tro")

Giuseppe Zanotti ("zje-sep-pe zah-not-tee")

Givenchy ("zshee-von-she")

Gucci ("goo-chee")

Gaultier ("go-tee-ay")

Hermès ("air-mez")

Hervé Legér ("air-vay lay-jay")

Issey Miyake ("is-ay-mee-yah-ke")

James Perse ("purse")

Jean Paul Gaultier ("go-tee-ay")

John Varvatos ("var-vay-toes")

Lanvin ("lon-vin")

Louis Vuitton ("loo-e vee-ton")

Maison Martin Margiela ("maze-on mar-tin mar-gel-a")

Marchesa ("mar-kay-sah")

Miu Miu ("mew-mew")

Moschino ("mo-skeen-o")

Narciso Rodriguez ("nar-see-so rod-ree-gez")

Monique Lhuillier ("mo-neek loo-leeyay")

Manolo Blahnik ("muh-no-low blah-nik")

Peter Som ("sahm")

Pucci ("poo-chi")

Proenza Schouler ("pro-en-za skooler")

Ralph Lauren ("laur-en," like the girl's name Lauren, not like Sophia Loren)

Rodarte ("ro-dar-tay")

Salvatore Ferragamo ("sal-va-tor-ray fair-a-gah-mo")

Sonia Rykiel ("ree-kee-el")

Thakoon ("ta-koon")

Theyskens ("tay-skins")

Tibi ("tib-ee")

Ungaro ("oon-gar-o")

Versace ("verr-sah-chay")

Yohji Yamamoto ("yo-jee ya-ma-moto")

Yves Saint Laurent ("eve san lor-on")

Zac Posen ("po-zen")

Zegna ("zen-yuh")

---

*As a general rule of thumb, only wear what you know how to pronounce, in the event someone asks who you're wearing.

## About the creators

**Stephanie Simons** is the author of *All's Fair In Love and Wardrobe*, the first dating rulebook for fashion lovers. An editorial strategist and television beauty expert based in the San Francisco Bay Area, her work has appeared in countless publications including *DailyCandy*, *InStyle*, and *Cosmopolitan*. She specializes in product naming and advertising campaigns for global retail brands and credits her linguistic talents to mom and dad, who made up all sorts of funny words and embarrassing nicknames for her growing up. Find her at facebook.com/allsfairinloveandwardrobe and on twitter @lovenwardrobe.

**Malia Carter** is the creator of DeepFriedFreckles.com, a popular illustration blog featuring fashion and celebrities and named after her favorite accessories: her freckles. Her watercolor illustrations have been featured by *Teen Vogue*, Kingsrowe Gallery, and numerous fashion blogs worldwide. She lives in Columbus, Ohio, where she carries her paintbrushes with her everywhere she goes. Find her at facebook.com/deepfriedfreckles and instagram.com/deepfriedfreckles.

Special thanks to Kristin Kulsavage at Skyhorse Publishing
for speaking our language.

And to Gretchen Weiners for trying to make *fetch* happen.